D1268899

Your Baby Girl

A collection by
BARTY PHILLIPS

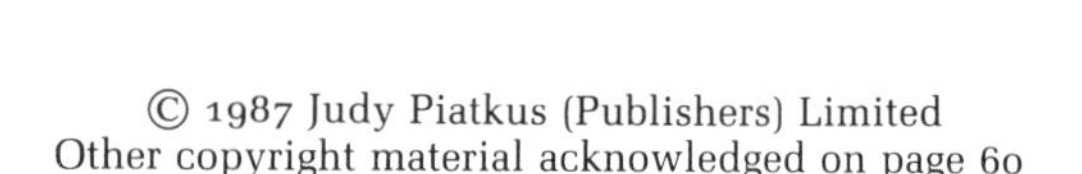

First published in Great Britain in 1987 by
Judy Piatkus (Publishers) Limited
5 Windmill Street, London W1P 1HF

British Library Cataloguing in Publication Data

Phillips, Barty
Your baby girl.
1. Infants
I. Title
305.2′32 HQ774

ISBN 0-86188-579-1

Drawings by Paul Saunders
Designed by Sue Ryall
Cover artwork by Sue Warne

Phototypeset in 9/11 pt Linotron Melior
Printed and bound at The Bath Press, Avon

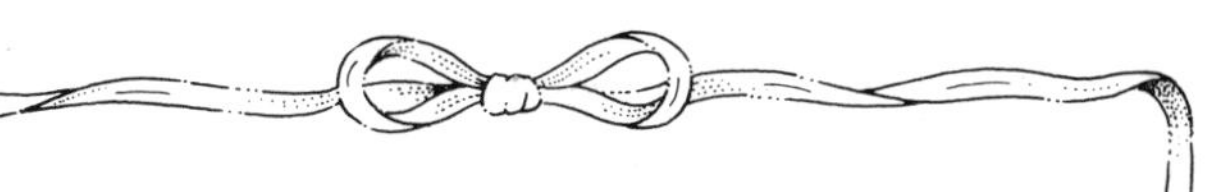

CONTENTS

NO PROUDER MAN

'No prouder man can be,
When in her eyes I see,
Sweet recognition glow.
It is a foolish thing I know;
For the Great Hand that wrought her
Made other babies so—
But this one is my daughter!'

Richard Churchill

BIRTH CEREMONIES

When a child is born, a community may concentrate on ceremonies which ward off evil (as in so many fairy tales such as Sleeping Beauty) or those which receive the child into the community, as in Christianity and other religions.

Primitive people often feel afraid of a magical unluckiness, so before birth they may make women taboo and isolate them in special huts. Sometimes there is a ceremony after birth of readmission to the tribe after the time of seclusion. Hopi Indian women are not allowed to go out until five days after the birth and in England there is a custom that the mother should not go outside afterwards until she has been 'churched'.

These taboos may apply to husbands too. In some places neither the husband nor the wife is allowed to approach a fire, eat fruit, bore holes or dive into water in case they injure the child. In South America, China and the Pacific Islands the father is put to bed when the baby is born, sometimes dressed as a woman as if he had had the baby. He may stay there for days or even weeks.

In Ancient Greece the father used to run round the hearth after the birth; in Estonia he ran round the church while the baby was being baptised. In parts of the Philippines the husband stands on the house brandishing a sword. Amulets and charms are often

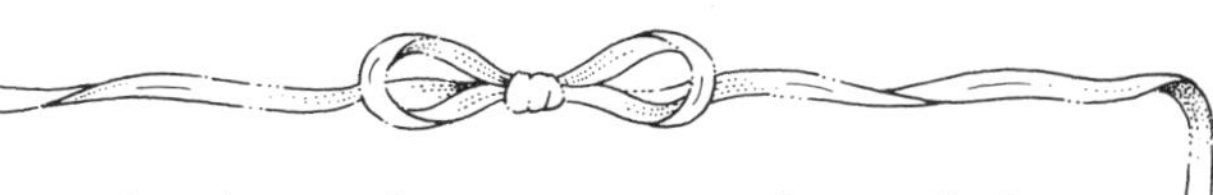

fastened to the new born to protect it from evil. A Navaho Indian child's life is marked by rituals. A flint is used to cut the umbilical cord and the woman who assists with the birth has the privilege of holding the child first. The baby is laid next to her mother with her head to the north and annointed with corn pollen —a symbol of life.

In the folk belief of nearly all the peoples of the world, the afterbirth is closely associated with the soul, life, death, health, character, success or failure of the child. What becomes of it determines the child's life. Some Indian tribes present a boy's afterbirth to the ravens so that he will see into the future; if it's a girl they bury the afterbirth at the high tide mark so she will become a good clam digger.

The Aymora Indians of Bolivia cover the afterbirth with flowers and bury it with cooking pots if it's a girl. In Java the women place the afterbirth in a little vessel, bedeck it with fruits, flowers and lighted candles and set it adrift in the river at night to please the crocodiles (who are supposed to be inhabited by the ancestors of these people).

Among certain tribes of Central Africa, the afterbirth is considered to be the actual twin of the child and is put in a pot and buried under a plantain tree, for that is where the ghost (or twin) lives. If anyone not related makes food or drink from this tree, the ghost will go away and the child will follow its twin and die.

WHERE DID YOU COME FROM?

Where did you come from, baby dear?
Out of the everywhere into here.

Where did you get those eyes of blue?
Out of the sky as I fell through.

What makes the light in them sparkle and spin
Some of the starry twinkles left in.

Where did you get that little tear?
I found it waiting when I got here.

What makes your forehead so smooth and high?
A soft hand stroked it as I went by.

What makes your cheek like a warm white rose?
I saw something better than anyone knows.

Whence that three-cornered smile of bliss?
Three angels gave me at once a kiss.

Where did you get this pearly ear?
God spoke, and it came out to hear.

Where did you get those arms and hands?
Love made itself into bonds and bands.

Feet, whence did you come, you darling things?
From the same box as the cherubs' wings.

How did they all just come to be you?
God thought about me, and so I grew.

But how did you come to us, you dear?
God thought about you, and so I am here.

George MacDonald

HISTORY OF BABY GIRLS

In pre-historic times women appear to have enjoyed a freedom unthinkable in classical times. And girls have by no means always had a good reception through the ages. In ancient Greece, a century before Aristotle, the woman wasn't even given credit for being the 'true' mother of a child, and according to the Egyptians, 'The father alone is true author of generation.'

Centuries later, in Italy, Da Vinci was more enlightened: 'The seed of the female is as potent as that of the male in generation' he said.

In parts of the world where the people depended on men to fight their wars baby girls were considered worse than useless since they couldn't fight and there weren't enough men left alive from the armies for them to marry. As babies they were often laid out on the bare hillside to die of exposure and starvation.

In ancient Sparta and Athens the aim of marriage was to produce an heir—and not too many of those, since numbers of children reduce a family's wealth. 'May you have no more than a single son to keep the patrimony together. That is the way to preserve wealth' wrote one Greek poet, Hesiod. 'Even a poor man will bring up a son, but even a rich man will expose a daughter,' wrote another Greek poet, Posidippus.

Up until the eighteenth century over half the

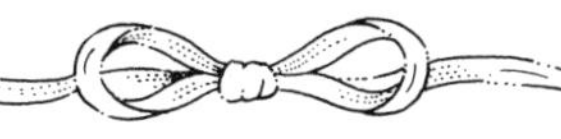

children born were dead before the age of five. Little wonder that parents should prevent themselves from becoming too fond until there was some reason to suppose the child would survive. Perhaps that's why it was so common for a mother to give a baby to its wet nurse for adoption from very early on. In 1585 the poet de Sainte Marthe wrote somewhat scornfully:

> But you, perhaps by other cares beguiled
> Wish, to the nurse's home to move your child
> Because by his continued cries at home,
> Your sleeps are broken and your jobs o'ercome.

Queen Anne, however, refused to let her child go to a wet nurse at all. 'Would I let my child, the child of a king, suck the milk of a servant, and mingle the royal blood with the blood of a servant?' she protested.

Young babies crying is nothing new. A household manual of 1765 devoted no less than four pages just to cradle-rocking and rich families used to employ an under nurse whose sole job was to rock the cradle. She was simply known as 'the rocker'.

One thing modern science has brought us is multiple births resulting from fertility drugs. During the eighteenth century however, the wife of Feodor Vassilyev who lived near Moscow needed no such drugs to give birth, during 27 confinements, to 16 pairs of twins, seven sets of triplets and four sets of quads, 69 children in all.

Modern techniques for caring for premature babies are very sophisticated nowadays, nevertheless when

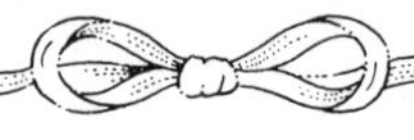

Marion Taggart was born on 5 June 1938 six weeks early and weighing just 10 oz her doctor found a way of keeping her alive: he fed her every hour for the first 30 hours with brandy, glucose and water through a fountain pen filler. At three weeks she already weighed 1 lb 13 oz and by her first birthday she weighed 13 lb 14 oz. By the time she was 21 she weighed 106 lbs and got married soon afterwards.

The first 'test tube' baby was Louise Brown, who weighed 5 lb 6 oz at her birth by Caesarian section at Oldham, Lancs, on 25 July 1978.

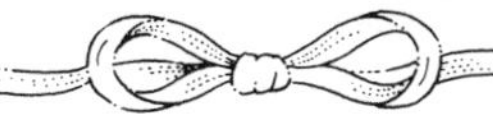

FAIRY TALE BABIES

Undine, the water nymph has become immortal in literature through the story by la Motte Fouque. She lived in the Rhine and longed to be a mortal. Her uncle Kuhleborn made a mighty storm and Undine, in the shape of a tiny baby, was washed to the shore of a lake where a couple of old fisher people who had lost their own child adopted her.

When she had grown up, a knight called Huldebrand rode through the forest and asked if he could lodge with the old fisher folk. That night another storm rose, the lake burst its bounds and encircled the house so they were cut off from land. A priest, wrecked below their hut, married them and Undine at once become mortal. The lake sank down to its usual size and they started a happy married life together, watched over by uncle Kuhleborn disguised sometimes as a waterfall and sometimes as a stream.

But jealous Bertalda, from Huldebrand's past, discovered them and created trouble. Undine, aware that Huldebrand was being seduced from her, had the castle well covered with a large stone so that none of her Rhine people could come and take revenge on her husband. Sure enough, Huldebrand was influenced by Bertalda and turned against Undine telling her to go back where she belonged.

Undine vanished over the side of the boat and melted like water into the stream. Huldebrand grieved

for a while but married Bertalda, who, to show her own mastery over the castle ordered the well to be uncovered. Then a pillar of water rose from it that changed into the shape of Undine, who, wringing her hands walked to Huldebrand's chamber where they found him dead in her arms. They buried him and a bubbling spring gushed from the turf by his grave, encircling it before it flowed into the lake. Thus Undine still embraces her beloved knight.

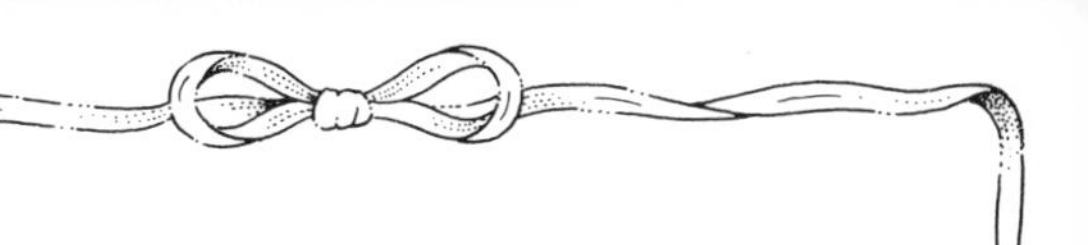

HUSH LITTLE BABY

Hush little baby don't say a word,
Papa's going to buy you a mocking bird

If the mocking bird won't sing
Papa's going to buy you a diamond ring.

If the diamond ring turns to brass,
Papa's going to buy you a looking glass

If the looking glass gets broke,
Papa's going to buy you a billy-goat.

If that billy-goat runs away
Papa's going to buy you another today.

Anon

STAR SIGNS

The sun passes through one of the twelve signs of the Zodiac each month. The simplest horoscopes are based on the position of the sun when a baby is born without taking the other planets into account. It is a rough and ready way of assessing character but often surprisingly accurate.

If the birthday falls in the middle of the Zodiacal period the baby will have strong characteristics of his or her sign. If it falls on either side, he or she will incorporate some of those belonging to the neighbouring sign.

The signs fall into four categories: Earth people are generally practical, Air people thoughtful, Fire people idealistic and Water people emotional.

21 March–20 April:  **ARIES THE RAM**

Fire sign. Colour, red. Aries is the symbol of spring. These people are pioneers in thought and action, brave, adventurous and fond of travel, though highly strung with a tendency to head and toothaches. Your child will be ambitious, self reliant, energetic and impulsive and will be walking almost before crawling. Will be loyal if treated well, act impulsively if dissatisfied. Full of schemes and ideas but has the urge to do things quickly. Anything needing patience or dedication will soon be abandoned. Your baby will

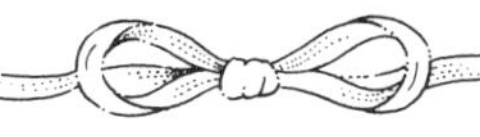

love to talk and may embroider on the truth just for fun. Arians often become designers, architects, writers or entertainers. Famous Arians include Pearl Bailey, Alec Guinness, Charlie Chaplin. Compatible signs are other Arians, Leos and Sagittarians.

21 April–21 May: TAURUS THE BULL

Earth sign. Colours, blue and pink. Taureans are pretty healthy on the whole: inclined to chest and throat ailments if anything. They often have good singing voices. Taurus indicates strength of character and purpose and a Taurus baby may be led but never driven and determined to the point of obstinacy. Such children need security, are slow to anger but have violent tempers when roused, though they are usually quick to forgive. They make good organisers and managers and are financially astute. Famous Taureans include Catharine the Great, Salvador Dali. Compatible signs are other Taureans, Capricorn and Virgo.

22 May–21 June: GEMINI THE TWINS

An Air sign. Colour, bright yellow. Gemini indicates a contradictory nature which makes such children elusive and rather unpredictable but they are very affectionate. They are adaptable and versatile and need constant variety. They seldom lose control and cope well in emergencies but find it difficult to

concentrate on one thing for any length of time, whether a project or a person. Famous Geminis include Judy Garland, Queen Victoria, Paul McCartney. Compatible signs are other Geminis, Aquarians and Librans.

22 June–22 July: CANCER THE CRAB

Water sign. Colour, violet. Cancerians respond to the changing influence of the moon but are also tenacious and obstinate. They are deeply moved by the fortunes of other people. They are conservative and home loving, liable to have romantic ideals. Such babies will be inventive and original, excellent mimics with good memories. They often surprise their families by being shy and possessive. They love comfort and good living which makes them grow up to become good cooks and homemakers. Eventually your child will probably veer towards the arts and will want to travel. Famous Cancerians include Gina Lollobrigida, Rembrandt. Compatible signs are other Cancerians, Pisces, Scorpios.

23 July–23 August: LEO THE LION

Fire sign. Colour, orange. Proud, ambitious, masterful, sincere and generous, Leo is the king of signs. Leos love everything big in life, are trusting and good hearted, practical and hard headed, with plenty of will-power and self control. Do not be surprised if

your child sets high goals for him or herself, particularly in controlling others rather than in manual skills. Typical careers might be as an orchestra conductor, organist, actor, mural painter—anything grand. Famous Leos include Princess Anne and Napoleon. Compatible signs are other Leos, Aries and Sagittarius.

24 August–23 September:  VIRGO THE VIRGIN

Earth sign. Colours, grey or navy. You can often tell Virgos by their rather prominent, aquiline noses. Your baby will grow up to have an analytical mind but a matter-of-fact façade may hide a nervous nature. Virgos may not show their feelings but nevertheless have strong ones.

They are rather exacting to people they are close to. They are shrewd and inventive with words, methodical and logical with a good eye for detail. They are also practical with their hands and make good technicians. Famous Virgoans include Queen Elizabeth I, Dr. Johnson and D. H. Lawrence. Your baby will make friends with other Virgoans, Capricorns and Taureans.

24 September–23 October:  LIBRA THE BALANCE

Air sign. Colour, indigo. Librans are charming, fun

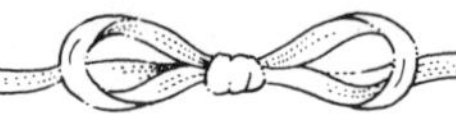

loving and appreciate beauty, elegance and harmony. They are impartial and fair, great observers, curious about people. Take care, your baby will listen carefully and pick up and take in everything you say including social gossip. The Libran's impartiality leads them to be arrogant in the belief that they can't be wrong and they often refuse to enter into arguments or discussions and absolutely hate quarrels. Famous Librans include Lady Jane Grey, Mahatma Ghandi. Compatible signs are other Librans, Aquarians and Geminis.

24 October–22 November: SCORPIO THE SCORPION

Water sign. Colour, deep red. This sign indicates a smooth surface with hidden depths. These people have very powerful natures, are calm and watchful but with magnetic intensity and can have a hypnotic influence over people. Your baby will be strong willed, determined, yet cautious, shrewd and self confident; will be very direct in giving opinions and sometimes quick to take offence. Nevertheless Scorpios make good friends, possessive and passionate lovers. They often become public speakers, detectives or doctors. Famous Scorpios include Katharine Hepburn, Mary Queen of Scots, Prince Charles. Compatible signs are other Scorpios, Pisces and Cancer.

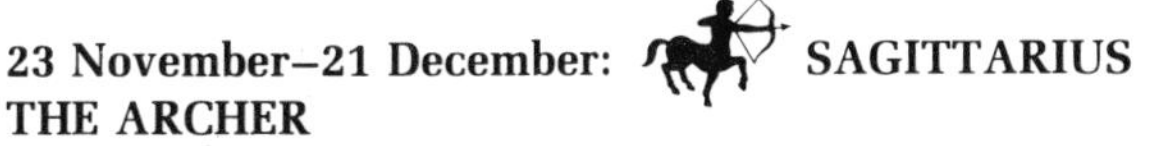

23 November–21 December: SAGITTARIUS THE ARCHER

Fire sign. Colour, light blue. Sagittarians are honest, optimistic, trustworthy and loyal but very independent and tend to be restless. Your baby will feel cramped by a play pen and will want to be exploring the world. They are natural teachers and philosophers though inclined to be outspoken and impulsive. They may be attracted to politics, teaching, law or religion. Famous Sagittarians include Jane Austen, Winston Churchill. Compatible signs are other Sagittarians, Arians and Leos.

22 December–20 January: CAPRICORN THE GOAT

Earth sign. Colour, green. Capricorn people are economical, practical, perservering, shrewd and diplomatic, though likely to rush into things and sometimes behave unexpectedly. Your baby will enjoy learning and arguing, will grow to enjoy being in authority in any chosen profession and will be a loyal friend and lover, though may decide to live alone. Other famous Capricorns include Joan of Arc and Mozart. Their most compatible signs are other Capricorns, Taureans and Virgos.

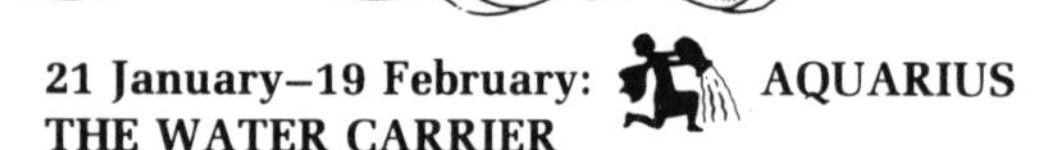

21 January–19 February: AQUARIUS THE WATER CARRIER

Air sign. Colour, bright blue. Your Aquarian will have an open, outgoing personality and an inquiring mind. Such children may have unexpected outbursts of temper, throwing their toys across the room in a fit of rage but at other times they are gregarious and fun loving. They have rather contradictory natures, being both idealistic and practical. They will have strong maternal instincts and love teaching. They are faithful and loving but expect a great deal of others. Interests are likely to be poetry, astronomy, music and entertainment. Famous Aquarians include Dame Edith Evans, Charles Dickens. Compatible signs are other Aquarians, Geminis and Librans.

20 February–20 March:  **PISCES THE FISH**

Water sign. Colour, sea green. At their best they are good natured, friendly and kind. Your baby will be quick to learn, have a vivid imagination, be interested in music and the arts, the mysterious and literature. He or she may lose confidence from time to time and need special comforting. Pisces people don't find it easy to concentrate and many follow two or more interests at once. Typical careers are as nurses, librarians or designers. Famous Pisceans include Elizabeth Taylor, Hans Christian Andersen. Compatible signs are other Pisces, Cancer and Scorpio.

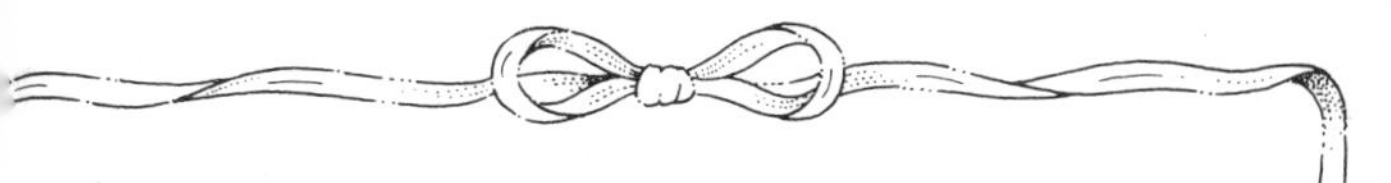

BIRTH STONES

Particular precious or semi-precious stones and particular flowers are supposed to bring luck to those born at certain times of year. Lucky stones for birth months are said to be:

JANUARY—Garnet (*constancy*): a semi-precious stone usually red, looking a bit like a ruby. It is said to make the wearer cheerful.

FEBRUARY—Amethyst (*sincerity*): a kind of quartz coloured purple or violet. In Greek it means to protect from being drunk. Lucky to lovers.

MARCH—Bloodstone (*courage*): a dark green semi-precious stone with red spots like small bloodstains. Soldiers used to wear it thinking it would staunch wounds.

APRIL—Diamond (*purity*): diamonds are water coloured and brilliantly sparkling. They should be worn on the left side and symbolise strength, virtue, courage and insight.

MAY—Emerald (*hope*): a beautiful green stone. The Romans believed it was good for the eyes which is why the Emperor Nero wore emerald eyeglasses.

JUNE—Agate (*health*): a semi-precious stone with stripes of colour usually brown, dark red or yellow,

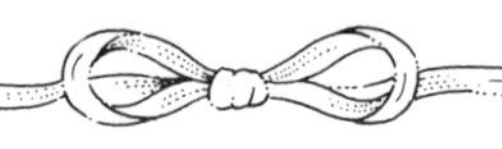

but sometimes blue or green. Lucky for foresters, farmers and gardeners. Good for friendship.

JULY—Ruby (*contentment*): a precious jewel similar to sapphire except in colour which can be deep glowing red or pink to almost violet. Assuages grief, brings good friendships.

AUGUST—Sardonyx (*fidelity*): a handsome stone, a type of onyx with white and dark red or dark brown markings in bands. Said to bring married happiness and protect from snake bites.

SEPTEMBER—Sapphire (*repentance*): a precious stone which, at its best is a clear cornflower blue. Lucky to lovers; brings peace and optimism.

OCTOBER—Opal (*loveableness*): a cloudy white stone with hidden rainbow colours when it catches the light. Known as the stone of tears because it is brittle and inclined to break. Gives second sight, hope and faith to those whose birth stone it is.

NOVEMBER—Topaz (*cheerfulness*): a more or less transparent precious stone usually of a clear yellow, though sometimes yellowish white, blue or pink. Supposed to ward off bronchitis and asthma and bring friendship and love.

DECEMBER—Turquoise (*unselfishness*): a sea blue, opaque precious stone whose colour and sheen vary depending on the mood of the wearer. Protects from danger and sorrow.

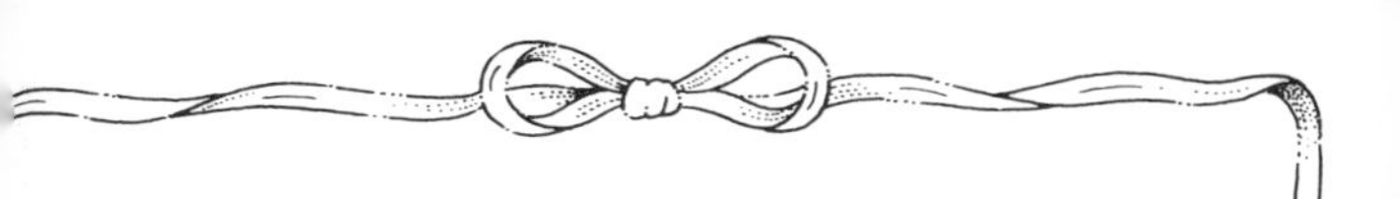

BIRTH FLOWERS

January—carnations and snowdrops
February—primroses
March—daffodils
April—daisies
May—lilies of the valley
June—roses
July—water lilies
August—gladioli
September—asters
October—dahlias
November—chrysanthemums
December—holly

TO OUR DAUGHTER

And she is beautiful, our daughter,
Only six months, but a person.
She turns to look at everything, out walking
All so precious. I mustn't disturb it with words.
People are like great clowns,
Blossom like balloons, black pigeons like eagles,
Water beyond belief.

She holds out her hand to air,
Sea, sky, wind, sun, movement, stillness
And wants to hold them all.
My finger is her earth connection, me, and earth.

Her head is like an apple, or an egg.
Skin stretched fine over a strong casing,
Her whole being developing from within
And from without: the answer.
And she sings, long notes from the belly or the
 throat,
Her legs kick her feet up to her nose,
She rests—laid still like a large rose.
She is our child,
The world is not hers, she has to win it.

Jennifer Armitage (from 'Bread & Roses' an Anthology of Nineteenth and Twentieth Century Poetry by Women Writers)

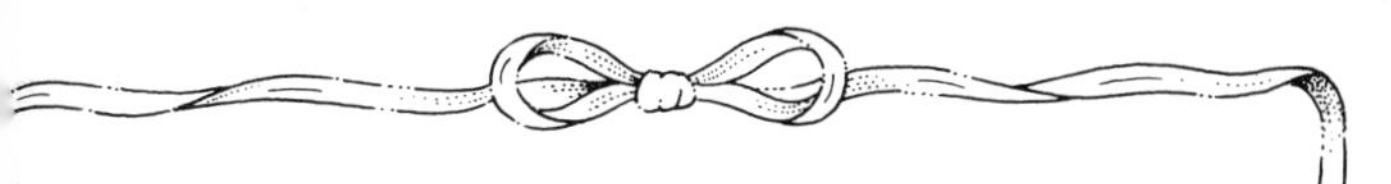

FOR A HEALTHY GIRL

People have always had strong feelings about upbringing. Among the earliest criticisms of the upbringing of a child is this one from the Bible: 'And as for thy nativity, in the day thou wast born, thy navel was not cut, neither wast thou washed in water to supple thee; thou wast not salted at all, nor swaddled at all.'

Ezekiel

Cleanliness was paramount for Florence Nightingale: 'Children are much more susceptible than grown people to all noxious influences. They are affected by the same things, but much more quickly and seriously; by want of fresh air, of proper warmth; want of cleanliness in house, clothes, bedding, or body; by improper food, want of punctuality, by dullness, by want of light, by too much or too little covering in bed or when up.'

As for diet, Francis Bacon in Shakespeare's time wrote 'Examine the true habits of diet, of sleep and of exercise: command rather a good diet than a frequent use of physic.'

Mrs Beeton was a stickler for fresh air and cleanliness: 'Frequent washing of the person, both of nurse and children, are even more necessary in the nursery than in either drawing-room or sick-room, inasmuch as the delicate organisms of childhood are

more susceptible of injury from smells and vapours than adults.'

In the 1920s Dr Truby King, who now has the reputation of being a tyrant over defenceless mothers, was considered very advanced in his thinking. He had a schoolmasterly way of putting his ideas across. He suggested giving infants a hard baked crust at eight months. 'The mother or nurse should take the child on her knee, hold the crust in his mouth and teach him to suck it; after a few days' perseverance the crust will become a treat.' (Note the 'he'.)

In 1931 bed wetting was put down to 'giving children liquids just before bedtime, worms, tight foreskin or a stone in the bladder.'

Culpeper in his Herbal advised the use of angelica which he said 'helps the pains of the cholic, the stranguary and stoppage of the urine, procureth women's courses and expelleth the afterbirth.' Ladies' Bed Straw 'decocted and used warm and the joints afterwards annointed with ointment, it helpeth the dry scab and the itch in children'. Caraway seeds 'bruised and fried, laid hot in a bag or double cloth to the lower parts of the belly, easeth the pains of the wind cholic.'

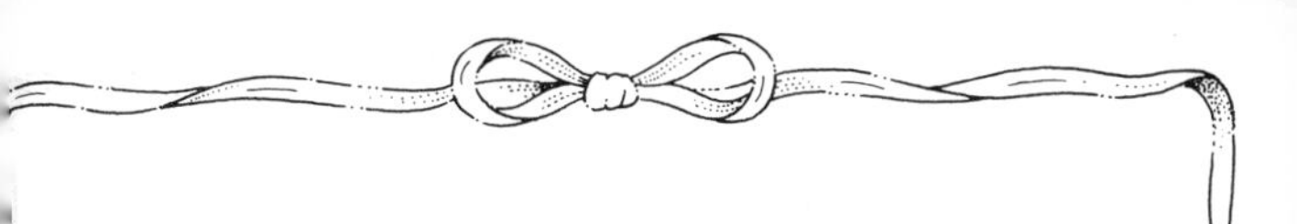

MONDAY'S CHILD ...

Monday's child is fair of face,
Tuesday's child is full of grace,
Wednesday's child is full of woe,
Thursday's child has far to go,
Friday's child is loving and giving,
Saturday's child works hard for a living,
But the child that is born on the Sabbath day
Is bonny and blythe and good and gay.

BIRTHMARKS AND SUPERSTITIONS

Giving birth has become a much safer process than in the past and it is no longer necessary to invoke magic spells to ensure a safe birth and a healthy baby. People still cling to some superstitions, though. It used to be widely believed (and in some countries still is) that a birthmark was the result of the mother having seen something unpleasant while she was pregnant, or even that she had been touched by some demon or other evil spirit during her pregnancy. Mothers were supposed to lick the mark for several days after the child was born, and indeed, spittle does seem to have had curative powers in some cases.

Birthmarks or strawberry marks were often useful as a proof that a baby was of royal blood, since the birthmark was often hereditary. On some of the Greek Islands such marks are known as 'the fating' or 'the fates'.

Moles are often signs of good luck, for instance a mole in the middle of the forehead or between the wrist and the elbow means money later on, while one just above the temple implies a person of wit and understanding. Moles on the chin, ear and neck, are lucky and the girl with a mole on her left breast will be irresistible to men. There are many other lucky omens: a German superstition says that if clouds are shaped like flocks of sheep or lambs at the time of

birth the baby will be lucky and in Yorkshire they say the baby should be carried to the top of the house so that it will 'rise in the world'. In some places it is the custom to show a child two objects (a violin and a purse, say) and the one it reaches for will indicate its future occupation.

Parents can take heart that a child who cries long will live long; a child born feet first (a 'footling') will have the power to cure muscular pains and become a local healer. A bald child will grow up to be a brilliant scholar, but a child weaned in Spring will become prematurely grey haired and a child born with teeth will be selfish (biting the breast that feeds it, no doubt).

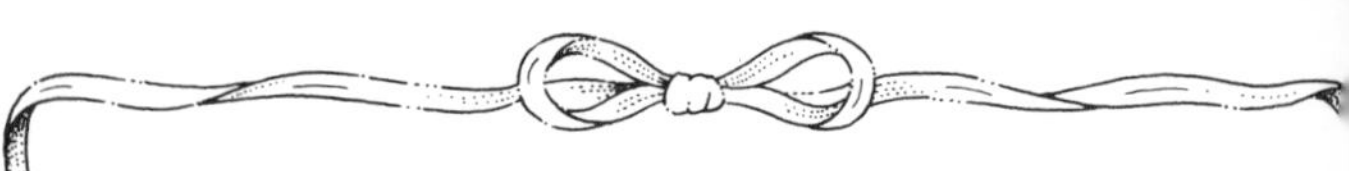

GRANDMOTHERS' TALES ON BRINGING UP GIRLS

'In every work the beginning is the most important part, especially in dealing with anything young and tender.'

Socrates

Common admonitions to little girls by their nannies in Victorian nurseries were 'silence is golden'; 'little girls should be seen and not heard'; 'ask no questions and you'll be told no lies' and the highest form of praise allowed was 'neat and tidy but not pretty' in case the child should become vain.

Education for little middle class Victorian girls was supposed to leave them with charming (but useless) accomplishments like playing the piano and painting watercolours.

Nannies were all powerful in the nursery. Even as recently as 1975, a London mother interviewing a prospective nanny was told: 'I will call you Mrs. Evans and you will call me nanny. You may come up to the nursery to see the baby in the evening and when you go on holiday with your husband baby will come and stay with me.'

Girl children were expected to sew and there are many samplers in existence which show how much time and patience was given to neat little stitches and very fine work, and also some incredibly fine darning

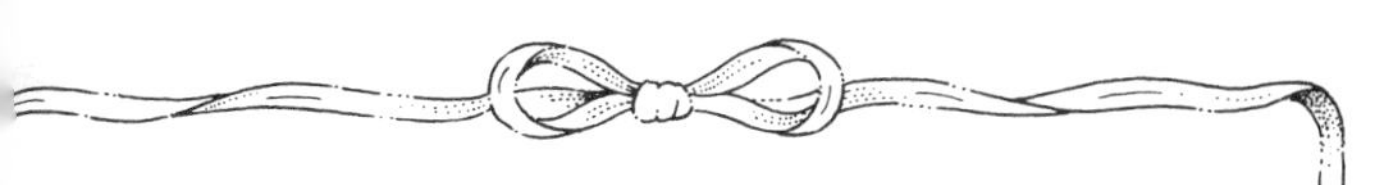

which most modern women would find hard to emulate. The phrase 'a stitch in time saves nine' was dinned into a little girl's head early on. Being 'bad' or 'good' was a part of Victorian childhood, mostly these were synonymous with being a nuisance or not. There were plenty of rhymes to impress the message such as:

'There was a little girl who had a little curl,
Right in the middle of her forehead.
When she was good she was very very good
But when she was bad she was horrid.'

Punishment and reward came into Charles Kingsley's *The Water Babies* too, in which two sisters have care of the babies under water: Mrs. Bedonebyasyoudid 'a very tremendous lady she was: and when the children saw her they all stood in a row, very upright indeed, and smoothed down their bathing dresses, and put their hands behind them, just as if they were going to be examined by the inspector. She had on a black bonnet, and a black shawl, and no crinoline at all; and a pair of large green spectacles, and a great hooked nose, hooked so much that the bridge of it stood quite up over her eyebrows; and under her arm she carried a great birch-rod. Indeed she was so ugly Tom was tempted to make faces at her, but did not; for he did not admire the look of the birch-rod under her arm.' Mrs. Doasyouwouldbedoneby was a very tall woman, but instead of being gnarly, and horny, and scaly, and prickly like her sister she was the most nice, soft, fat, smooth, pussy, cuddly, delicious creature who ever

nursed a baby and all her delight was, whenever she had a spare moment, to play with babies, in which she showed herself a woman of sense; for babies are the best company, and the pleasantest playfellows in the world; at least, so all the wise people in the world think. And therefore when the children saw her, they naturally all caught hold of her, and pulled her till she sat down on a stone, and climbed into her lap, and clung round her neck, and caught hold of her hands; and then they all put their thumbs into their mouths, and began cuddling and purring like so many kittens.'

But in the main children were expected to keep quiet and do as they were told, and indeed families were so large that unless there were plenty of nursemaids and servants there was only one way to deal with them which was the way of the old woman who lived in a shoe:

> Who had so many children
> She didn't know what to do.
> She gave them some broth
> Without any bread
> And whipped them all soundly
> And sent them to bed.

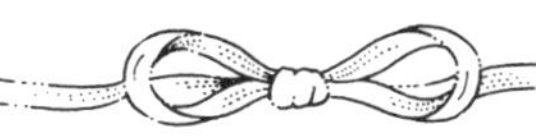

SWADDLING

When the child is born
He must be swaddled.
(Treatise of Walter de Biblesworth)

Swaddling was the rule in Europe from the early Middle Ages to the early nineteenth century, but it was already coming in for severe criticism by some of the medical profession in the eighteenth century.

Swaddling consisted of bandaging the baby's body over a cloth, a shirt or some other small garment. It was the custom to bind the whole infant, with its arms down by its sides, until four months so that it resembled a tight little parcel. That was thought to protect its fragile limbs and made it a bundle that was easy to carry. The swaddling bands might be wrapped in a criss-cross pattern or from top to toe in a single spiral band. Over the swaddling an upper-class baby would be dressed, possibly in a taffeta coat with satin sleeves, a bib and a gathered apron with strings and a necklace. The arms and hands were freed after a few months, but the torso, belly and feet were to be swaddled for a year.

Swaddling slowed down the infant's metabolism so that it didn't need changing often and seldom cried.

Dr. William Cadogan in 1748 was among the first to condemn the practice: pointing out that 'the Child is so cramp'd .... that its Bowels have not Room, nor the Limbs any Liberty, to Act and exert themselves in the

free easy manner they ought ... I would recommend the following Dress: A little Flannel Waistcoat without Sleeves, made to fit the body, and tie loosely behind; to which there should be a Petticoat sew'd, and over this a kind of Gown of the same Material, or any other, that is light, thin and flimsy.'

To those of us blessed with disposable nappies and stretch baby clothes, swaddling seems outlandish. But in primitive and agricultural societies it does have advantages and babies are still swaddled in some parts of the world.

For instance each Navajo Indian father traditionally makes a 'cradleboard' for his newborn infant to which the baby is virtually swaddled. When the baby is put into it everybody chants this song:

'I have made a baby board for you my daughter
May you grow to a great old age
Of the sun's rays I have made the back
Of black clouds I have made the blanket
Of rainbow I have made the bow
Of sunbeams I have made the side loops
Of lightening I have made the lacings
Of raindrops have I made the footboard,
Of dawn have I made the bed covering.
Of black dog have I made the bed.'

In this cradleboard, the baby can be strapped to his mother's back, stood upright against a tree, or tied to a saddle horn, leaving her free to continue with her work while her baby remains safe and quiet.

HUSH—OH HUSH!

'Hush—Oh hush! my little wild one,
Hear the stirring in the hollow,
With thy restless little crying
Thou wilt wake the small sea-swallow.
Dearer than the bread of raupo,
Dearer than the sweet konini,
Dearer than the dead to Tane,
Yea, so dear art thou until me.
Sleep, my wild karaka berry,
Sleep, my red-lipped rata-blossom,
Ate! Ate! Ate! Ate!'

Eileen Duggan (Maoriland)

HISTORY OF THE BABY CARRIAGE

Baby carriages of one sort or another have been used for centuries. In Athens a clay model of a baby cart has been dug up and there is pictorial evidence of their use in fourteenth-century India and Ceylon.

Britain seems to have caught on to the idea rather late on, presumably relying on nursery maids until the nineteenth century when wooden baby carriages were made for the very rich. Those built for Lady Georgina Cavendish at Chatsworth were adult coaches in miniature and very elaborate. In the 1840s experiments were made with various designs including three wheelers, carriages to be pulled, some to be pushed and the first patent was taken out by Charles Burton in 1853 for 'The Perambulator'. In 1853 he opened a showroom in Oxford Street with four other manufacturers. Queen Victoria bought three Burton carriages.

Early British 'prams' were pretty dangerous, having no springs and arsenic-coated harnesses. They also gave an opportunity for nursemaids to neglect their small charges. However, many had considerable grace and beauty, with liveried wood casings surrounded by minature balustrades, lined with buttoned leather and trimmed in gleaming brass. Bassinet versions (popular in the USA and colonies) were reed woven in shell-coiled arabesques with parasols or canopies

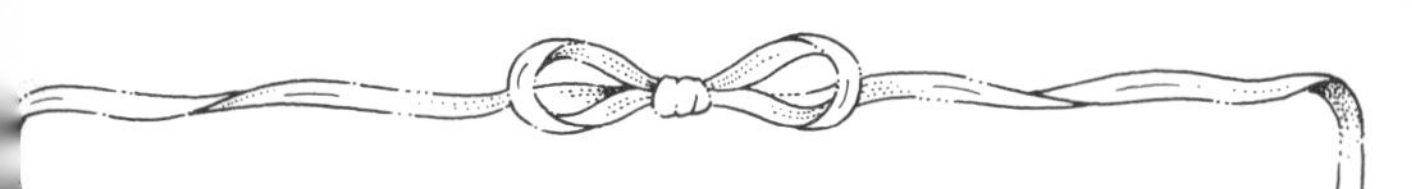

fluttering overhead to keep off the sun. Eventually, simpler, two-handled carts were developed, like those which postmen had been using. They were cheaper and lighter, easier to manoeuvre and dashingly designed. Eventually they became upholstered, with attachments across the handles to allow babies to lie full length.

By the 1900s baby carriages had become very sophisticated. Double hoods meant that two babies could be housed in all weathers, and carriage lanterns on the mudguards allowed the nurse to go for extended walks far into the twilight or fog. Mothers were only very occasionally to be seen wheeling *their own* prams: 'a crucial test of your moral courage and innate ladyhood' said one mother of the time.

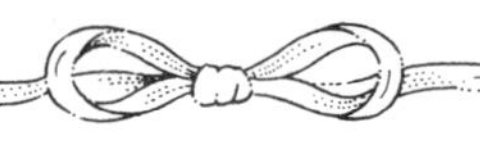

SINGING AND TALKING GAMES

A parent who talks frequently and closely to a baby with eye contact and pronounced lip movements will be much more likely to find the baby talking back and responding. Singing and talking games are a time honoured way of encouraging babies to respond and of helping them to grasp the meanings of words. Such games are very important as an introduction to communication. Babies love to have these games repeated over and over again and that is how they learn.

There are many rhymes to demonstrate parts of the body.

For instance here's one for the face:

Here sits the Lord Mayor (forehead)
Here sits his men, (eyes)
Here sits the cockadoodle, (right cheek)
Here sits the hen, (left cheek)
Here sit the little chickens, (teeth)
Here they run in (mouth)
Chin chopper, chin chopper,
Chin chopper, chin.

And several for the fingers:

Thumbikin, Thumbikin broke the barn,
Pinnikin, Pinnikin, stole the corn,
Long back'd Gray carried it away,
Old Mid-man sat and saw,
But peesy-weesy paid for a'.

Thumb he
Wizbee
Long man
Cherry tree
Little jack-a-dandy.

Little Pig
Phillimore
Grimthistle
Pennywhistle
Great Big Thumbo
Father of them all.

And a favourite one for the toes:

This little pig went to market,
This little pig stayed at home,
This little pig had roast beef,
This little pig had none,
And this little pig cried
Wee Wee Wee Wee, all the way home.

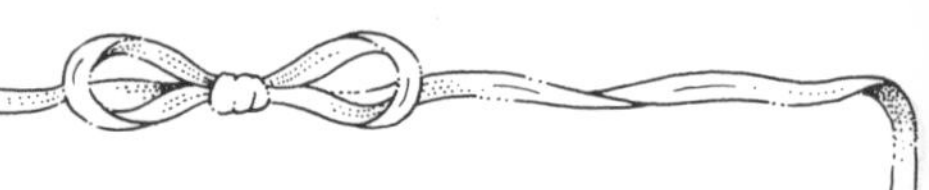

Tickling games:

Round and round the garden [palm of the hand],
Like a Teddy bear;
One step, two step
And tickly under there [the armpit].

Round about, round about, here sits the hare
In the corner of a cornfield and that's just there
[by the thumb].

This little dog found her
This little dog ran her
This little dog caught her
This little dog ate her
And this little dog said 'Give me a little bit
please.'

Knee rides and dandling:

And another great favourite with babies is this:

This is the way the ladies ride,
Trit trot trit trot trit trot trit trot;
This is the way the gentlemen ride
gallopy, gallopy, gallopy, gallopy
This is the way the farmers ride
Trot trot trot trot trot trot trot trot.
This is the way the ploughboys ride
Hobble dee hobble dee hobble dee—and DOWN
into a ditch.

Babies still love knee rides of which these are among the best known:

Dance to your daddy,
My little babby,
Dance to your daddy,
My little lamb.

You shall have a fishy,
In a little dishy,
You shall have a fishy
When the boat comes in.

You shall have an apple
You shall have a plum,
You shall have a rattle basket
When your daddy comes home.

In Scotland, there's a slightly different version:

Dance to your daddie,
My bonnie laddie,
Dance to your daddie,
My bonnie lamb.
And ye'll get a coatie,
And a pair of breekies—
Ye'll get a whippie
And a supple tam!

FIRST TOYS

For the first few months what a baby needs most of all is contact with people. Objects are meaningless at this stage. Her best 'toys' are listening to her parents' voices and studying their faces and she will love to be picked up and held closely.

From four to five weeks your baby will begin to experience where her body ends and the world begins. She will enjoy watching mobiles, will like the sensation of a warm bath and will begin to take notice of rattles or toys strung across her baby carriage.

From about twelve weeks baby will begin to want to hold things. This is the time when rattles begin to come into their own and when she will begin to discover that she has some control over creating rattling noises. Babies are attracted by bright colours and enjoy learning about shapes so a variety of rattles is a good idea: also woolly balls, well-sealed plastic bottles with different objects inside to make different sounds will all be of interest. Dried peas, paper clips, sand, all make different sounds.

Some babies can swing and jump happily from baby bouncers usually hung from a strong hook in the doorway. If the ceiling is high enough, baby can bounce on the table where she will enjoy being on a level with you.

From about six months babies will have fun playing with household objects, a toothbrush, saucepan and

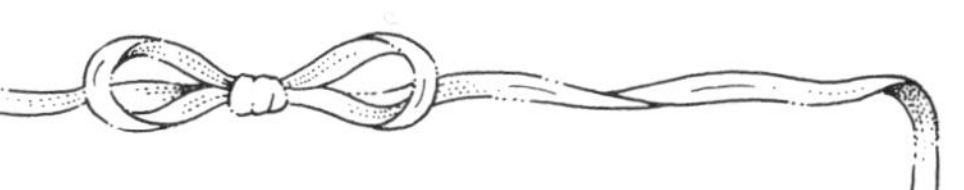

wooden spoon, own spoon and beaker, toys with wheels, toys that squeak when squeezed, paper to tear. An activity centre attached to the cot bars may encourage her to play quietly early in the morning before you have woken up.

Balls to roll (marbles are too small and get popped into small mouths), bricks, toys to experiment with in terms of texture and behaviour (biscuits crumble, bread is squashy, apples are smooth and hard). Ping pong balls can be rolled down a cardboard tube, a xylophone makes interesting sounds.

At the crawling stage your daughter will love big-wheeled toys, cushions, enormous Teddy bears, big balls and will be fascinated by seeing her own face in a mirror.

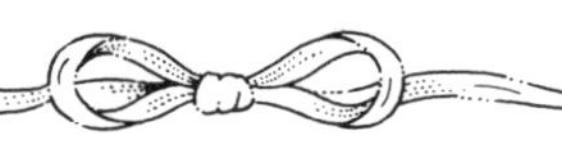

LITTLE GIRL

I will buy you a house
If you do not cry,
A house, little girl,
As big as the sky.

I will build you a house
Of golden dates,
The freshest of all
For the steps and the gates.

I will furnish the house
For you and for me,
With walnuts and hazels
Fresh from the tree.

I will build you a house
And when it is done,
I will roof it with grapes
To keep out the sun.

Arabian nursery rhyme

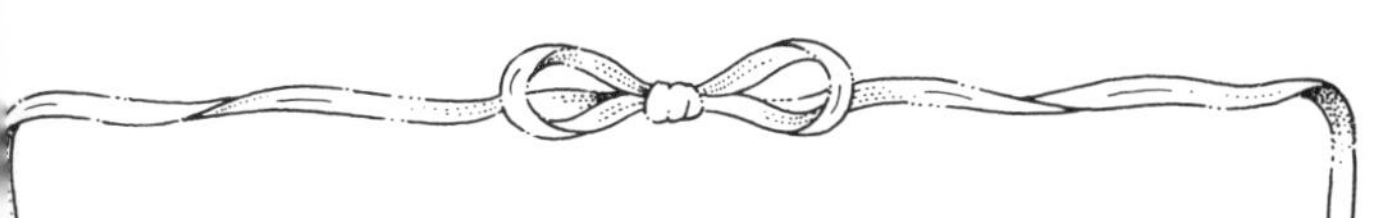

THINGS TO MAKE

First baby carriage toy

Babies like brightly coloured objects strung along the front of the baby carriage. For these little balls use five different bright colours of felt and stuff them with kapok or old (but clean) tights cut up small.

Each ball is made of four segments. Draw a line 3 in long and across the middle of it draw a line $1\frac{1}{2}$ in long. Now draw a curve from one long end to the other, touching each end of the short line. Cut out the segment shape in thin card. From this template you can cut as many segments of felt as you need. If you want to embroider the felt, do it now. Join the pieces together using oversewing. Leave the last two sides open. Ease the stuffing in, pressing it into shape. Sew up the opening. Cut two small circles or flower shapes. Punch a hole in the centre of each and glue or stitch over the joined points. Thread elastic through, using a bodkin. Five of these strung together will be enough to stretch across the baby carriage.

First mobile

Babies love to watch things move, lying in a baby carriage out of doors they will delight in watching the leaves waving in the breeze and the clouds racing by. A very simple mobile can be made by cutting thick coloured card into simple shapes and hanging them from a wire coat hanger, or hang from it a variety of different small objects; a shiny spoon, a cotton reel, a plastic duck, all at slightly different heights. Place it where she can see it while lying in her cot, but where she can't reach up and grab it as she grows older.

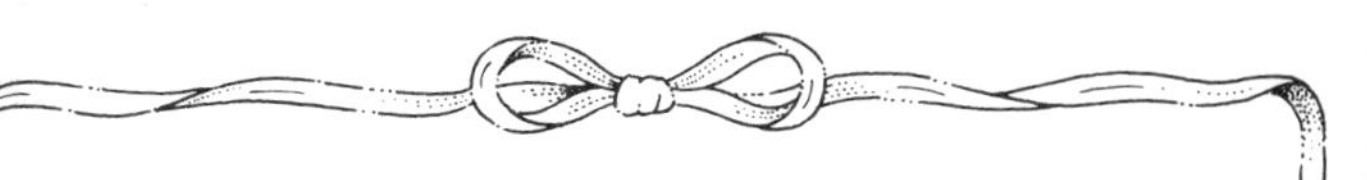

NAME CEREMONIES

In many societies the baby's name has a spiritual importance and must be chosen with great care. Eskimos say that a person is made up of body, soul and name, the name being the part which survives death.

One common idea is that a baby is an ancestor reborn. The parents must discover the ancestor's name, rather than choose their own name for the baby. This is done by holding the baby up while it is crying. and repeating a list of family names. When the baby stops crying—that is its name.

In some places the parents are considered virtually 'impure' for ten days after the birth and are kept in isolation. On the tenth day the child is given a public name and the impurity of the parents is ended.

There is often a fixed date after the birth for the name-giving ceremony. In ancient Greece it was the Tenth Day. In South Germany it was thought that the soul flew about between rebirths in the form of a butterfly. In China a new-born babe is presented before the gods and communion established between it and its ancestor.

Baptism of one sort or another is common in many communities including Central Asia and Tibet. Running water which purifies is considered good for birth ceremonies. In Britain it is supposed to be unwise to tell the baby's name before the Christening as fairies or evil spirits might steal it.

Arthur Grimble describes an experience which illustrates the power of a name when he was based on one of the Gilbert Islands in the early 1900s. 'No white baby had ever been seen before on Tarawa. The villagers seemed never tired of looking at Joan's blue eyes and golden hair. One evening a small naked girl in the crowd mustered to gaze around the pram piped aloud "Ai bia aran te tei-n-aire aie!" (I would that this girl-child's name could be my name). I said "What's all the fuss about? Why shouldn't she?" I turned to Olivia: "Of course she may," she said: "What's to stop it if the mother likes it?" There was a shout of pleasure from the audience. The mother, looking her thanks, led her small girl to the side of the pram and, bending over it, addressed our sleeping Joan with a smile of tender courtesy: "Neiko (Woman), I have thrown away the name of this, my girl child, and taken your name for her instead. Your mother says I may. See, here is your name-sister and servant for evermore, Joan of Betio, who shall obey your word in all things."'

Arthur Grimble from *A Pattern of Islands*

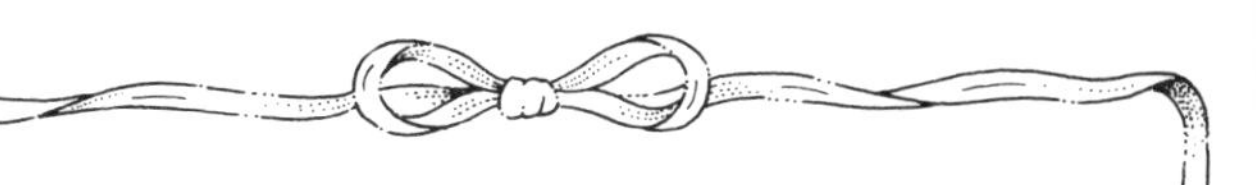

NAMES AND MEANINGS

Children may be named after places or given their parents' surnames but often a name reflects the joy a baby has given her parents and some of these names are given here.

ABIGAIL: *father's joy* (Hebrew)
AGNES: *pure* (Greek)
AMANDA: *lovable* (Latin)
AMY: *beloved* (Old French)
ANGELA: *an angel* or *a messenger* (Greek)
ANN, ANNE, ANNA: *grace* (Greek and Hebrew)
ANTHEA: *flowery* (Greek)
AVRIL: *April* (French)

BEATRICE: *bringer of joy* (English and Italian)
BERENICE: *bringer of victory* (Greek)
BERTHA: *the shining one* or *the bright one* (Norse)
BLANCHE: *fair, pure* (Old French)
BRIDGET, BRIDGIT, BRIGID, BRIGIT: *tall, stately* (Irish from St Bride)

CAMILLA: *noble maiden fit to serve in a temple* (Latin)

CANDIDA: *white* (Latin)

CARA: *friend* (Irish); also *dear girl* (Italian)

CARMEL: *vineyard* or *fruitful garden* (Hebrew)

CASSANDRA: *helper of men* (Greek)

CATHERINE: *pure* (Greek)

CELIA: *heavenly* (Latin)

CHLOE: *a green and tender shoot* (Greek)

CLARE, CLAIR, CLARA: *renowned* (Latin)

CORA: *a maiden* (Irish and US)

DEBORAH: *a bee* (Hebrew)

DIERDRE: *the raging one* (Old Celtic)

DORIS: *goddess of the sea* (Greek)

DOROTHEA: *gift of God* (Greek)

DULCIE: *sweet* (Latin)

EDITH: *prosperity* and *warlike* (Old English)

ELIZABETH, ELISABETH: *consecrated to God* (Hebrew, Greek, Latin)

ELVINA: *friendly* (Celtic)
EMILY: *rival* (Roman)
ENID: *spotless purity* (Old Celtic)
ESME: *love, value* (French)
EUNICE: *good victory* Greek)
EUPHEMIA: *fair speech* (Greek)
EVA: *life giving* (Hebrew and Latin)
EVELEEN: *pleasant* (Celtic)

FELICITY: *happiness* (Latin)
FENELLA: *white shoulder* (Celtic)
FIONA: *white* (Gaelic)
FLEUR: *flower* (French)
FLORA: *flower* (name of the Roman goddess of flowers and spring)
FLORENCE: *flourishing* (Latin)

GLORIA: *fame* (Latin)
GWYNETH: *blessed* (Welsh)

HANNAH: *He has favoured me* (Hebrew)
HEBE: name of the Greek goddess of youth

HILARY: *cheerful* (Latin)
HONOR: *honour* (Latin)

IANTHE: *violet flower* (violet flower)
INGRID: *fair one* (Norwegian)
IRENE: *peace* (Greek)
IRIS: *rainbow* (Greek)

LETITIA: *gladness* (Latin)
LYNN: *a pool* (Celtic)

MARGARET, MARGET, MARGARETTA: *a pearl* (Greek)
MARIBELLE: *lovely* (French)
MARTHA: *a lady* (Greek and Latin)
MARY: wished for child (Hebrew and Latin)
MAVIS: *song thrush* (Old French)
MELANIE: *black* (Greek)
MELISSA: *sweet* (from the Greek for *bee*)
MERLE: *blackbird* (French)
MINNA: *very small* or *kind thought* (Germanic)
MOIRA: *soft* (Celtic)

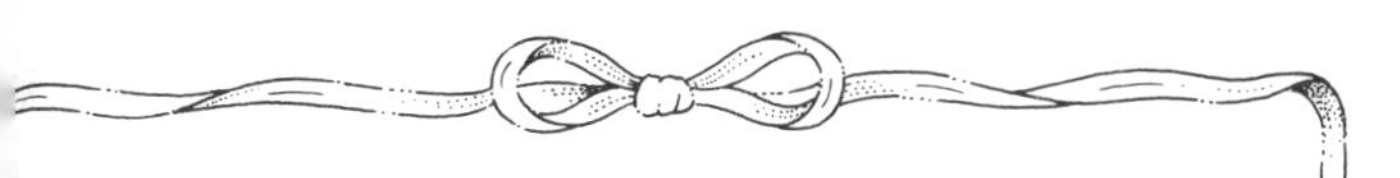

MONICA: *unique* or *stand fast* (Greek)
MURIEL: *sea bright* (Irish from Muirgheal)
MYFANWY: *child of the water* (Welsh)

NADINE: *hope* (Russian)

PERPETUA: *everlasting* (Latin)
PHOEBE: *radiant* (Greek, describing the Moon Goddess)

REGINA: *a queen* (Latin)
ROSALIA: *rosy* or *rose like* (Latin)

SABRINA: earliest known name for the river Severn
SALOME: *peace* (Hebrew and Greek)
SARAH, SARA: *the princess* (Hebrew)
SELINA: *heaven* (French or Latin)
SERENA: *serene* or *untroubled* (Latin)
SONIA: *wisdom* (Russian)
SOPHIA: *wisdom* (Greek)

STELLA: *a star* (Latin)

SUSANNAH (Hebrew), **SUSAN** (English), **SUZANNE** (French): *lily*

SYBIL, SIBYL: *prophetess* (Greek and Latin)

SYLVIA: *wood* (Latin)

TARA: *hill* (Irish)

URSULA: *she-bear* (Latin)

VANORA: *white wave* (Celtic)

VERA: *faith* (Russian)

VICTORIA: *victory* (Latin)

VIOLA: *the violet* (Latin)

WINIFRED: *peaceful friend* (Old English)

ZOE: *life* (Greek)

ZORA: *dawn* (Arabic)

BORN YESTERDAY

Tightly-folded bud,
I have wished you something
None of the others would:
Not the usual stuff
About being beautiful,
Or running off a spring
Of innocence and love—
They will all wish you that,
And should it prove possible,
Well, you're a lucky girl.
But if it shouldn't then
May you be ordinary;
Have, like other women,
An average of talents:
Not ugly, not good-looking,
Nothing uncustomary
To pull you off your balance,
That unworkable itself,
Stops all the rest from working.
In fact, may you be dull—
If that is what a skilled,
Vigilant, flexible,
Unemphasized, enthralled
Catching of happiness is called.

Philip Larkin

MY JEWEL

God keep my jewel this day from all danger;
From tinker and pooka and black-hearted stranger;
From harm of the water, and hurt of the fire;
From the horns of the cows going home from the byre;
From teasing the ass when he's tied to the manger;
From stones that would bruise and from thorns of the briar;
From evil red berries that waken desire;
From hunting the gander and vexing the goat;
From cut and from tumble, from sickness and weeping;
May God have my jewel this day in His keeping.

W M Letts

Timely blossom, Infant fair,
Fondling of a happy pair,
Every morn and every night,
Their solicitous delight,
Sleeping, waking, still at ease,
Pleasing, without skill to please;
Little gossip, blithe and hale,
Tattling many a broken tale,
Singing many a tuneless song,
Lavish of a heedless tongue;
Simple maiden void of art,
Babbling out the very heart,
Yet abandon'd to thy will,
Yet imagining no ill,
Yet too innocent to blush;
Like the linnet in the bush
To the mother-linnet's note
Moduling her slender throat;
Chirping forth thy petty joys,
Wanton in the change of toys,
Like the linnet green, in May
Fitting to each bloomy spray;
Wearied then and glad of rest,
Like the linnet in the nest:—
This thy present happy lot,
This, in time will be forgot:
Other pleasures, other cares,
Ever-busy Time prepares;
And thou shalt in thy daughter see,
This picture, once, resembled thee.

A Philips *To Charlotte Pulteney*

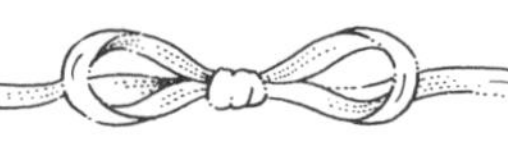

COUNSEL TO GIRLS

Gather ye rose-buds while ye may,
Old Time is still a-flying:

And this same flower that smiles to-day,
Tomorrow will be dying.

The glorious Lamp of Heaven, the Sun,
The higher he's a-getting
The sooner will his race be run,
And nearer he's to setting.

That age is best which is the first,
When youth and blood are warmer;
But being spent, the worse, and worst
Times, still succeed the former.

Then be not coy, but use your time;
And while ye may, go marry:
For having lost but once your prime,
You may for ever tarry.

Robert Herrick

IF NO-ONE EVER MARRIES ME

If no-one ever marries me—
And I don't see why they should;
For nurse says I'm not pretty,
And I'm seldom very good—

If no-one ever marries me
I shan't mind very much;
I shall buy a squirrel in a cage,
And a little rabbit hutch.

I shall have a cottage near a wood,
And a pony all my own.
And a little lamb quite clean and tame
That I can take to town.

And when I'm getting really old,
At twenty eight or nine,
I shall buy a little orphan girl
And bring her up as mine.

Laurence Alma-Tadema

HUSHABY

Hushaby, by, sleep little dove,
Core of my heart, content thee.
Hushaby, by, little prince of love,
Blessed be he who sent thee.

Italian lullaby

ACKNOWLEDGEMENTS

The publishers would like to thank the following authors (or their estates) and publishers for copyright material reproduced within this anthology:

Arthur Grimble and John Murray (Publishers) Limited for the extract from *A Pattern of Islands* on page 46;

Jennifer Armitrage and Virago Press for the poem *To Our Daughter* on page 22;

Philip Larkin and Marvell Press for the poem on page 53.